SAVE SOIL

Abhijit Ghosh

First Published in December 2022

ISBN: 978-93-5704-485-1

BLUEROSE PUBLISHERS
www.BlueRoseONE.com
info@bluerosepublishers.com
+91 8882 898 898

Cover Design:
Abhijit Ghosh

Typographic Design:
Pooja Sharma

Distributed by: BlueRose, Amazon, Flipkart

Contents

Introduction To Save Soil

Soil is a legacy. It is a gift from God on which our lives thrive.

As Charles Kellogg said, *"Essentially, all life depends upon the soil... There can be no life without soil, and no soil without life; they have evolved together."*

Within the natural world of soil, there exists a complex balance among living organisms. Plants, animals, and microorganisms—each plays a crucial role in life. Even if one of them fails, the whole ecosystem gets affected. However, when everything is in order, the outcomes are beautiful.

We have to save soil to give our future generations a better life. Our soil is degrading faster than we comprehend. As per the UN report, 40% of the soil is already degraded, and by 2050, 90% of fertile soil will not be fit for cultivation. And by then, the world population will be around 9 billion. There will be an acute food shortage and starvation. People will have to migrate from one place to another. According to the stark claims, only 60 years or less remain before it reaches the alarming level. Even though these figures are said to have a less scientific base, sometimes overblown, soil degradation is the important problem.

Topsoil is a living thing made up of countless microorganisms. An average of three feet of earth is covered with topsoil, the layer of dirt that provides the nutrients for most of the planet's land vegetation, biodiversity and is crucial for producing food from agriculture. Good topsoil improves crop yield. It is protecting the soil from degradation. This topsoil is getting eroded due to multiple factors such as unplanned farming, overgrazing, uninhibited urbanization, industrial waste, and many more hazardous conditions like water sheet erosion and wind blowing (storm). The problem only arises when soil erodes at an accelerated rate and cannot be replenished quickly enough. 40% of the topsoil has already eroded. It takes around 40–45 years to replenish topsoil and bring the soil to an accepted level of fertility.

It is undoubtedly a serious issue that will continue to increase in stature if changes are not implemented quickly. It is no longer a drawing room subject for discussion or the virtual programme in a seminar or symposium, where everything is kept aside after the meeting is over. To save soil, each of us must take positive steps by contributing something, which may include notifying our local authorities about the emergency.

This planet is our habitat, our home, and we must act quickly to prevent soil degradation.

We have to save the soil.

It is not only for us, but for our future generations as well.

Read on.....

SAVE SOIL

Save Soil is a global movement to encourage a conscious approach to saving our soil and planet.

This is predominantly a people's movement. The objective is to demonstrate the support of over 3.5 billion people (more than 60 percent of the world's population) around the world and to empower governments to initiate policy-driven action to revitalise soil and to prevent its further degradation. World leaders, influencers, artists, experts, farmers, spiritual leaders, NGOs, and citizens are vocally supporting the movement to re-establish humanity's relationship with soil and Mother Earth.

This global movement was launched by Indian spiritual master Sadhguru to address land degradation and advocate for healthy soil. It aims to get citizens of the world to emphatically express to their leaders the urgent need to save soil in their countries.

The Movement comes in the wake of the alarming degradation of fertile soils across the world, posing a clear and present threat to global food and water security. In India, nearly 30% of fertile soils in the country have already become barren and are incapable of yielding.

Sadhguru propelled the Movement to Save Soil in March 2022 to prevent the occurrence of soil degradation that UN agencies are referring to as "soil extinction" — the death of fertile soils is universal and is posing an existential threat to the human race.

Sadhguru emphasised..

"Food doesn't come from Uber Eats, it comes from soil". The healthier the soil, the healthier your food, the healthier your body".

SAVE SOIL

Right now, the most important aspect of conserving nature is the soil. If we do not stop soil degradation, the planet will not be conducive for human beings to live upon.
- SADHGURU.

Then what can be done to save the soil?

Sadhguru's suggested "start local, involve your neighbourhood, start a vegetable garden, get your hands in the soil—not in the dirt, as is commonly said, as soil is not dirty—it is rich. It is our foundation for a healthy life and a safe environment."

Honestly, the Isha Foundation's movement in the advancement of Save Soil has been supported by-

IUCN (International Union for Conservation of Nature).

SAVE SOIL

Eighty-seven percent of life forms on this planet - microbes, worms, insects, birds, animals, human beings, plants, trees and every other vegetation on the planet is sustained by an average of thirty-nine inches of topsoil. And that is in grave danger right now. In the last forty years, forty percent of the world's topsoil has been lost.
-SADHGURU

What is soil and why does it need saving?

Soil is a blend of minerals, organic matter, air, water, and living organisms. In order to sustain life, we need healthy soil.

Soil feeds the population.

95% of the food that we eat is the product of healthy soil. Without lots of healthy soil, it would not be possible for farmers to produce food for us.

It is the soil that feeds the population. The rate of soil degradation is alarming. We think soil will remain cultivable as long as humanity lives. It is not true. One-third of the world's arable lands has already degraded. The situation becomes even more alarming when we find that it can take a thousand years for just one centimetre of topsoil to regenerate.

Soil prevents droughts and floods

With the help of soil organisms, organic matter, and good soil management, healthy soils can store and absorb water. This makes them a vital resource for protecting against flooding and droughts.

A single hectare of soil has the potential to store and filter enough water for 1,000 people for one year.

SAVE SOIL

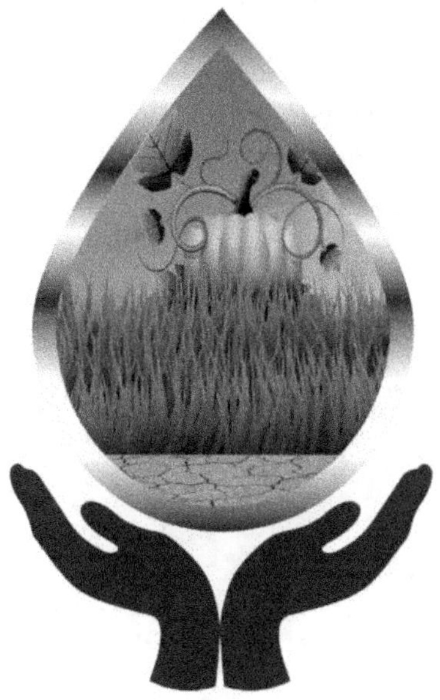

If we have any love for our children, we have to leave our soil and water in a better condition than they are now.
-SADHGURU

Soil combats climate change.

Healthy, well-managed soils capture carbon dioxide and store it as soil organic carbon. This makes them a vital resource in reducing our greenhouse gas emissions and confronting climate change.

For our climate, nature, and health, we need to step up our action on soil health as a matter of urgency. Here are the seven ways to be considered for progress and highlight the positive change.

Save Soil to save environment and earth.

Make it a global movement.

SAVE SOIL

GROW VEGETABLES

If there is no richness in soil, there will be no richness in life. Unless we do something significant in the next two decades, there will be a big price to pay.

- SADHGURU

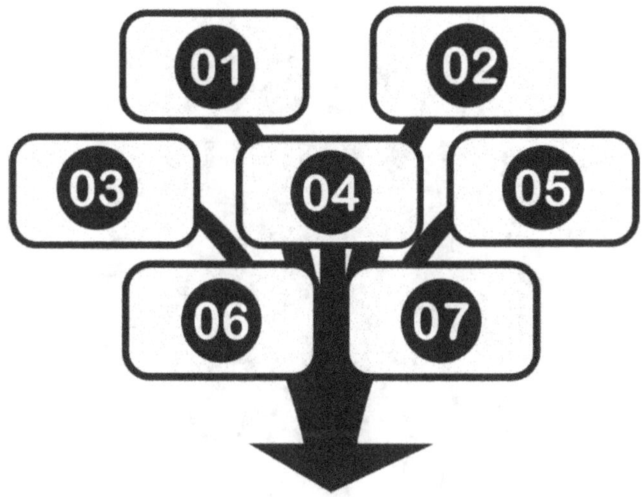

7 Steps to monitor soil health, which brings positive change.

1. Monitor Soil Health On Farms

2. Enhance The Return Of Plant And Animal Material To Fields.

3. Improve Soil Life By Reducing Tillage And Chemicals.

4. Cover Up Bare Soil With Continuous Plant Cover.

5. Bring More Trees Onto Farmland.

6. Reduce Soil Compaction From Machinery And Livestock.

7. Soil Health Benefits From Crop Rotation.

SAVE SOIL

Our body is essentially soil and water. The quality of our soil and water determines the quality of our food, our body, and our life.
- SADHGURU

Revitalization Of Soil

Sadhguru: 87% of life forms on this planet—microbes, worms, insects, birds, animals, people, plants, trees, and every other type of vegetation on the planet—is sustained by an average of 39 inches of topsoil.

This topsoil has been degraded. In the last forty years, 40% of the world's topsoil has been lost.

As per the United Nations estimate, we've got soil left for just close to a hundred harvests, which implies another forty-five to sixty years of agriculture. After that, we'll not have enough soil to supply food.

This implies great suffering for not only mankind but also for every living thing on earth.

30% of India's land is already degraded. 90% of India's state soil is going to turn into desert, which means nothing can be cultivated there. Saving soil for our future generations has to be treated as a top priority.

In the case of air pollution, it can be fixed in a short time. But fixing the soil, which has been degraded due to prolonged random usage, will take 15–25 years if we go aggressively. But if we go without much interest, then it may take 40-45 years to bring the soil to a certain level for cultivation.

SAVE SOIL

AGROFORESRY

Only because human beings are not living according to their human nature, they have to think up good things and they think of these good things which are unbearable for lots of people.
- SADHGURU

5 Methods That Can Revitalize Soil

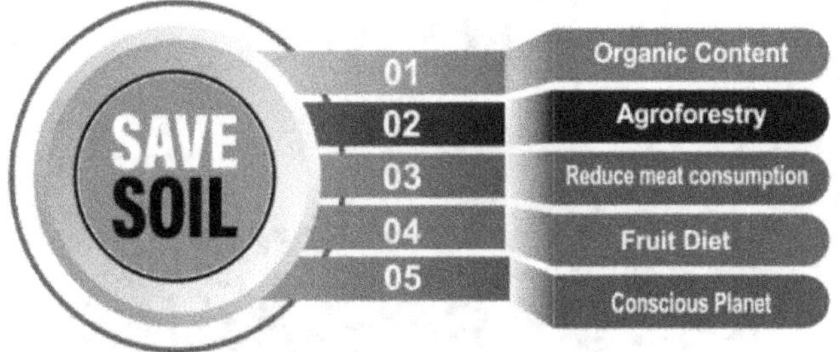

1. Organic Content Builds Healthy Soil

People have been cultivating the same land for thousands of generations. And progressively, the soil quality of the land has been degraded to a great extent. The condition of the soil is such that it is on the verge of turning into a desert. To improve the soil quality, organic components must go into it. Trees have to be planted and some animals have to be present in the soil.

This can replenish the top soil in its original form.

Trees, plants, and animals are needed to build healthy soil. Soil has to be covered to protect it from sand dust during storms and to avoid topsoil getting washed away during rain. 33% of the soil must be under shade to preserve the soil quality.

With a little support and protection, the soil will bounce back to its original form and give us a bountiful harvest.

SAVE SOIL

We must impart to every human being that soil, water, and air are not resources to be used and thrown away. These are life-making ingredients.

- SADHGURU

2. Tree Based Agriculture or Agroforestry

Agroforestry is the attempt to plant trees in farmlands alongside conventional crops.

Although there is no such thing as forest produce, agroforestry can definitely protect farmlands from erosion during sand storms and washing away fertile land during rainy seasons.

Agroforestry has multiple other benefits too. It is profitable for farmers. It re-establishes the ecological balance in farm lands and averts soil erosion and water wash away. It provides alternative income options. The timber available to the farmers can be productive and well-paid as well.

Agroforestry moderates extreme weather conditions such as sand storms, heavy rains, and floods and protects the soil from getting eroded.

3. Reducing Meat Consumption

Agriculture is practised on nearly 40 million square kilometres of land worldwide, of which 77% is used for raising animals for human consumption. It reduces the amount of arable land available for farming. If meat consumption is reduced by 50%, more land will be available for farming. This will help to enrich the soil conditions.

The farmers will be benefited. This will be good for our health. Even doctors suggest eating less meat for health reasons

SAVE SOIL

Every worm, every insect, every animal is working for ecological well being of the planet Only human being who claims to be most intelligent being species here, are not doing that.

\- SADHGURU

4. Fruit Diet- Good for You and the Environment

Our body contains 70% water, and doctors say if there is sufficient water content in the body, it is more manageable. They even suggest eating fruit during illness. If vegetables are eaten regularly, about 70% of water is supplemented in the body. Fruit has more water. If we eat fruit regularly, 90% of the water is added. We become healthier.

5. Building a Conscious Planet

40% of our soil is already degraded. It is high time we should be concerned about the degradation of soil and do something positive to save soil. The Save the soil movement led by conscious planet by Sadhguru is generating enough impetus in this respect.

Billions of Martian locusts can damage our trees, dry out our rivers, and damage our land enough to make deserts. We could be wiped out by them. It is not only the locusts that are the problem. Since humans are also causing soil degradation through irresponsible handling of the soil, they have to find a solution to save soil through a conscious planet approach.

It is the top 39 inches of topsoil that sustains most of the living organisms, including worms, insects, and animals, as well as human beings, on the earth. If this topsoil is managed properly by keeping this organically rich and healthy content, this planet will be capable of regenerating itself to a great extent. Ecological balance will take place and all other issues will be managed.

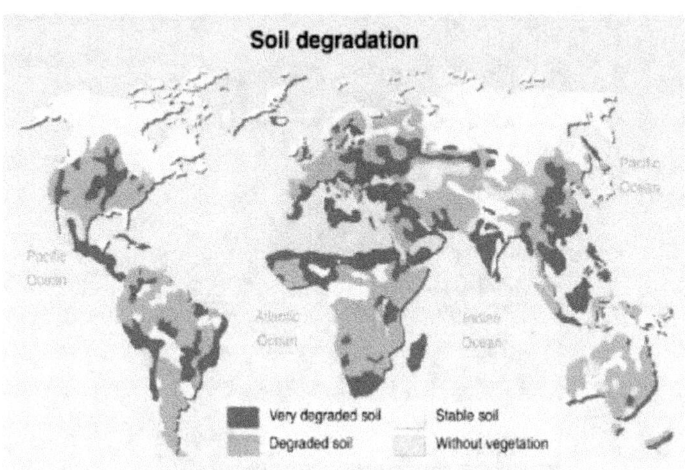

Source: UNEP International Soil and Information Centre (ISRIC). World Atlas of Desertification (1997)

SAVE SOIL

The earth is the basis of our life. Spending time touching the soil, plants, or trees will harmonize your system.
- SADHGURU

Conservation Of Soil

Soil conservation is the prevention of the loss of topsoil from erosion or reduced fertility caused by over usage, acidification, salinization, or other chemical soil contamination. Slash-and-burn and other unsustainable methods of subsistence farming are often carried out in some less developed countries, which contribute to soil erosion.

Deforestation is one of the major factors in soil erosion, loss of nutrients, and sometimes total desertification. The plants become soil when they die. The improved methods to prevent soil erosion and to maintain the fertility of the soil include crop rotation, crop cover, conservation tillage, and planted windbreaks.

Farmers have been following soil erosion techniques for ages. Political and government intervention will be more effective in addressing the soil erosion problem.

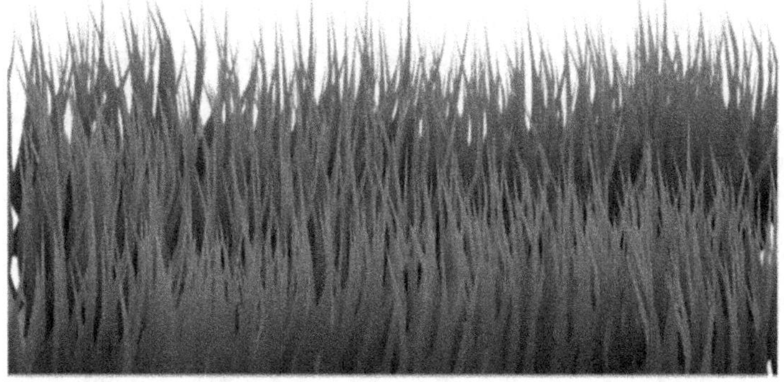

SAVE SOIL

PLANT TREES

The Soil is the soul of all the life upon this precious Planet. Soil is the very Conundrum of life and death. The only Magic material that turns death into life. The Magic of Soil, the basis of all riches of life we see. Depleting Soils can unleash the unfed gastronomic fire to burn and annihilate the very world. Let us not turn this Magic into Tragic.

\- SADHGURU

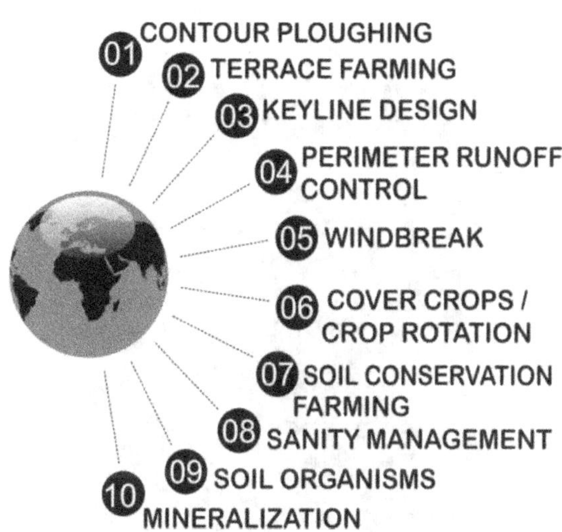

1. Contour Ploughing.

In contour ploughing the natural contours when tilling the soil, planting and cultivating are followed. It reduces the crop damage caused by floods, storms, and landslides by reducing soil erosion. By controlling runoff water, increasing moisture infiltration and retention, it improves soil quality and composition.

This ploughing method prevents soil erosion in hilly and contoured areas by capturing the water runoff.

SAVE SOIL

SAVE OUR PLANET

We are the environment. We are an extension of this earth. The ingredients of life are packed into the Air that we breath, Water that we drink, Sunlight and Soil.

- SADHGURU

2. Terrace Farming

Terrace farming is the practise of cultivating crops on the sides of hills or mountains by planting them on graduated terraces carved into the slope. A series of steps, each at a higher level than the previous form of terraces. Terraces are safeguarded from erosion by other soil barriers. Terraced farming is a more common practice on small farms.

It is an ingenious and ancient method of growing crops on steep, hilly slopes. A series of successive levels of flat surfaces along the slope of hills that resemble the steps of a ladder are constructed down the hill for farming.

Terrace farming increases farmability and productivity of the soil on slopped surfaces.

It contributes to water conservation, reduces water runoff, and improves rainwater harvesting.

It averts soil erosion.

3. Keyline Design/Technique

The Keyline Technique is adopted for maximising the water resources on a tract land. It is a wide-ranging and whole-farm water management plan. It uses natural landscape contours and cultivation techniques to harvest rainwater and build soil fertility.

P.A. Yeoman, an Australian person, invented it to capture water from a dwindling water supply and to prevent soil erosion in Australia. The key idea is to capture the water at the highest possible point and allow it to flow down outward using gravitational forces along the ridges.

The flow of water is maximised by allowing it to flow towards drier ridges using contour ploughing.

It prevents soil erosion.

SAVE SOIL

For me, action is about a solution, not about satisfaction. If we do not do the right stuff for Soil now, large-scale suffering will happen.

- SADHGURU

4. Perimeter Runoff Control

Perimeter runoff control is the most effective way to control soil erosion. Shrubs, trees, and grass ground cover are used as perimeter treatments for impending surface flows. Perimeter or inter-row treatment by the use of a grass way in both channels is used to dissipate runoff through surface friction.

It impedes surface runoff and assists infiltration of the slowed surface water.

SAVE SOIL

Agricultural practice that are Soil-friendly are vital for the future of Humanity. The Human Body is a reflection of the Living Soil.

- SADHGURU

5. Windbreak

A windbreak is also called a hedge, a hedgerow, a shelter belt, a vegetative barrier, or a wind barrier.

It can be identified as a fence, wall, line, or growth of trees that prevents the wind from coming through with its force.

Windbreaks are shrubs and plantings of trees linearly. It is designed to enhance crop production, protect people and livestock, and benefit soil and water conservation. Windbreaks are able to provide valuable opportunities for vine and tree fruit growers, row crop farmers, livestock producers, and rural homeowners.

SAVE SOIL

A large part of India's land which was one of the world's most fertile, is on the verge of becoming desert. 40% of India's soil will become uncultivable in 25 years unless we take positive action now.
- SADHGURU

6. Cover Crops

Cover crops are plants that are planted to cover soil. It is not used for the purpose of being harvested.

Cover crops reduce soil erosion, increase soil fertility and improve soil quality. Water, weeds, pests, diseases, biodiversity, and wildlife in an agro-ecosystem—an ecological system that can be managed and that is often shaped by humans. Cover crops are mostly an off-season crop planted after harvesting the cash crop. They are generally grown over the winter.

Cover crops can provide good soil cover. Its dense root system helps to stabilise soils and combat erosion. Clovers, annual ryegrass, winter peas, crown vetch, sudangrass, sorghum-sudan hybrids, rapeseed, mustards, and cowpeas are good cover crops for soil erosion protection.

7. Soil Conservation Farming / No Till Farming

In soil-conservation no-till farming is involved. It is also known as "green manure." It is soil-enhancing practises by which soil degradation can be minimised. Such farming methods are used on unfertile lands. They can revitalise damaged soil, minimise erosion, and encourage plant growth. It eliminates the use of nitrogen fertiliser or fungicide and can produce above-average yields.

SAVE SOIL

The body that carry is soil. Without the soil
being rich and well every other life cannot be
Well
Earth provides enough to satisfy every man's
needs but not enough every man's greed

- SADHGURU

It can protect crops during droughts or flooding. Repeated ploughing degrades soil, killing its beneficial fungi and earthworms. Even when all precautions are taken, it takes multiple seasons to fully recover from soil damage.

The no-till technique reduces equipment, fuel, and fertiliser needs, and the time required for tilling is also less. The method enhances soil-aggregate formation, microbial and invertebrate activity in the soil, and water infiltration and storage. No-till farming and cover crops drop nitrogen and other nutrients into the soil. The amount of organic matter is thus increased.

SAVE SOIL

Soil extinction is not just another ecological challenge. It is an existential threat. If we do the right things now, we can significantly turn this situation around and regenerate the soil in the next 15-25 years.

- SADHGURU

8. Salinity Management

Salinity management is maintaining the salt content in the soil. It is triggered by irrigation with salty water. When water evaporates from the soil, it leaves the salt behind. Salt breaks down the soil structure, which affects infertility and reduces growth.

Salinity takes place on dry lands from over irrigation and in areas where there are shallow saline water tables. Over-irrigation deposits salts in the upper layer of soil as a by-product of soil infiltration. Over-irrigation merely increases the rate of salt deposition. Salinity decreases plant growth and water quality, resulting in lower crop yields and degraded stock water supplies. Excess salt affects the productivity of soil.

It kills plants, leaving bare soil that is prone to erosion.

The primary method of controlling soil salinity is to permit 10–20% of the irrigation water to seep into the soil, so that it will be drained and discharged through an appropriate drainage system. Managing salinity involves striking a balance between the volumes of water entering (recharge) and leaving (discharge) the soil and having a proper groundwater system. Growing salt-tolerant plants used as negative vegetation is also effective in salinity management.

SAVE SOIL

Soil is the source of food, we eat. Food is the basis of our body. But some call this soil as dirt. If this source is dirt, then what of the end product? Only preserving the quality of the soil, the quality of the planet and life will endure.

- SADHGURU

9. Soil Organisms

Any organism inhabiting the soil during part or all of its life is a soil organism. Bacteria, fungi, and protozoa are mostly found in soil microbial processes. They perform many different kinds of functions which are beneficial to the soil and the plants growing in that soil. Besides these, there are other types of soil organisms such as nematodes, arthropods, and earthworms.

Soil microbes or microorganisms are tiny living things that are found in soil. They are sometimes too small to be seen by the naked eye. Besides soil, they can also be seen in the open air, water, and even in the human body. Some microbes are good for health; some make us sick, like viruses.

They increase soil fertility by adding air, minerals, and nitrogenous compounds. They facilitate increased plant growth by offering essential elements and minerals to plants.

Microorganisms decompose organic matter into a simpler form that can be easily accepted by plants.

SAVE SOIL

It is the time agriculture becomes the prime and lucrative activity in the country. If you do not make it a lucrative process in next 25 years we lose our ability to grow food in this country.
- SADHGURU

10. Mineralization

Mineralization is the process by which chemicals present in organic matter are decomposed or oxidised into inorganic forms that are available to plants. The transformation of organic molecules in soil is mainly driven by its microbiota, such as fungi and bacteria, and also earthworms. Active mineralization of the soil is sometimes undertaken to allow plants full realisation of their phytonutrient potential.

This can include adding crushed rock or chemical soil supplements. In either case, the purpose is to resist mineral depletion. A wide range of minerals can be used, including common substances such as phosphorus, etc. More exotic substances such as zinc and selenium are also sometimes used.

Flooding can generate significant sediment on an alluvial plain. While this effect may not be desired if floods endanger life or if the sediment originates from productive land, the process of the addition of sediments to a floodplain is a natural process that can rejuvenate soil chemistry through mineralization.

SAVE SOIL

Without reversing soil degradation, there is simply no way to reconcile the rapid decline in food production with the exponential growth in population size. This is our greatest generational prerogative and most valuable legacy.
- SADHGURU

Diagram of Soil Conservation

SAVE SOIL

Healthy soil is the basis of all Life on the planet.
Without addressing the immediate need to
preserve the organic content of our soil, food
security will inevitably come under severe threat.
- SADHGURU

Policies And Activities Related To Save Soil

The Save Soil movement has gained momentum after the founder of Isha Foundation, and a spiritual master, Sadhguru, set off on a lone 100-day motorcycle ride through 26 nations to raise awareness about soil degradation and losses of soil fertility over a period due to irresponsible cultivation, over-ploughing, unregulated deforestation, industrial pollution, etc. He has advocated for bringing organic content into agricultural processes.

WHO, the UN SDG lab, and the IUCN have all endorsed his movement.

Soil degradation is the physical, chemical, and biological degradability of soil quality. Half of the world's soil is already degraded because of unabated deforestation and urbanization, industrial pollution, overgrazing, and unsustainable agricultural malpractices. The loss impedes food quality and supply, water security, and biodiversity, and intensifies carbon emissions and climate related risks that can lead to loss of livelihood, conflict, and migration. The need for change in proper farming practises has become more urgent.

SAVE SOIL

ENCOURAGE PLATATION

Living Soil, our very body, is moving towards extinction. Addressing this with utmost urgency is the most important responsibility that all nations have to fulfil.

- SADHGURU

In recent years, IUCN (International Union for Conservation of Nature) has developed a new arrangement in agriculture and land health with the objective of implementing a common vision to protect and restore biodiversity on farms, including the ecosystems on which agriculture depends. Government, business houses, and land managers, including farming communities, are made to participate in this venture. The "Common Ground" from the IUCN report has displayed how soil and landscape biodiversity can benefit society and help overcome major challenges.

IUCN has offered to support its member, the Isha Foundation, in the advancement of the Save Soil movement to:

Draw the world's attention to degraded soils; Inspire 3.5 billion people (60% of the world's population) to support policy redirections to safeguard, nurture, and sustain soils; and Drive national policy changes in 193 nations to raise and maintain soil organic content to a minimum of 3-6%.

POLICIES AND ACTIVITIES RELATED TO SAVE SOIL

52

POLICIES AND ACTIVITIES BASED ON SHARING

When we think of economy, we look at the stock market and a few other things. But sixty-five percent of our population is in rural areas. If we just double their income, our economy will go through the roof.
- SADHGURU

Biodiversity is constantly under threat, and it is crucial to human wellbeing. Destruction of habitat, invasive species, over-exploitation, unlawful wildlife trade, pollution, and climate change have put the survival of species worldwide at risk. IUCN's global efforts to halt the extinction crisis and to sustainably manage, conserve, and restore ecosystems are laudable. They offer the methodologies, data, and expertise to guide decision makers and conservation action, using approaches that benefit nature and people's lives and livelihoods.

IUCN has worked towards a sustainable future for people and nature for the last 70 years. Recently, **Nature 2030**, an IUCN Programme, has for the first time set its ambitions in a decadal time frame (2021–2030). The IUCN works to protect the ecosystem by promoting sustainable land use and advancing conservation of justice and equity. Over the next decade, IUCN's 1400+ government agencies, Indigenous people, NGO's, its network of 16000+ scientists, and its secretariats will collectively mobilise the **Nature 2030** agenda to uphold its commitment to act for Sustainable Development Growth, Progress, and Biodiversity Framework Post 2020, work on based on the Paris Agreement on climate change, and including global recovery from pandemic due to COVID 19.

POLICIES AND ACTIVITIES RELATED TO SAVE SOIL

Our biological mother is only representative, the real mother is the soil – that we carry as body.

If we fix the soil, everything is fixed!! Water is fixed, air is fixed!

- SADHGURU

IUCN five has five transformative programmes, by which they have plans to achieve these decadal plan.

RECOGNIZE: IUCN has a plan to recognise and promote a collective understanding of the consistent challenges the world is facing. It has the determination and chronological order of what can be done about it and the role each actor can play, including governments, non-governmental organizations, academia, indigenous peoples, communities of women, and youth. It has vowed to recognise the incredible nature of the champions at all levels of nature and has committed to performing at all levels by working endlessly to protect and restore already degraded biodiversity.

RETAIN: Understanding the importance, IUCN has pledged to retain to safeguard, maintain, and sustainably use the world's biodiversity and natural and cultural heritage in key biodiversity areas and other intact areas.

RESTORE: IUCN is going to restore the condition of species and ecosystems and the full set of benefits that have been provided to people by nature that have already been lost or degraded, relying on the UN Decade of Ecosystem Restoration programme.

RESOURCE: The movement will be resourced from funding and investing in nature and the people working to conserve it, through finance, capacity development, and knowledge, to support humanity and the planet through both conventional and innovative initiatives.

RECONNECT: IUCN will assist in reconnection between people and nature to build a culture of conservation. This alignment is not just people with the planet, but through nature, with other individuals, communities, and their own heritage.

IUCN upholds strategies that integrate the sustainable management of land, water and biodiversity with human health and well-being. Tools like the IUCN Red List of Threatened Species, the IUCN Red List of Ecosystems and the Integrated Biodiversity Assessment Tool to inform conservation projects, business, national and international policy are assimilated. IUCN's aim is to conserve and restore species and ecosystems, and secure the ecosystem services on which humanity depends.

POLICIES AND ACTIVITIES RELATED TO SAVE SOIL

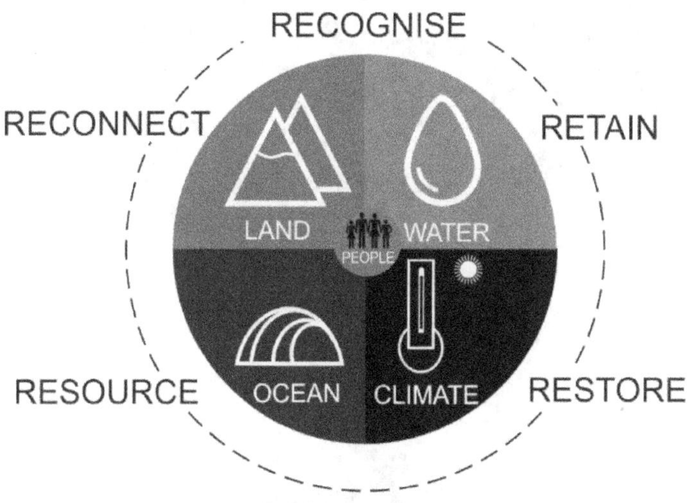

IUCN's Nature 2030 Programme Framework

POLICIES AND ACTIVITIES RELATED TO SAVE SOIL

Erosion And Degradation Of Soil

What is soil erosion?

Soil erosion is the process of wearing out the surface layer, or topsoil, caused by the movement of the surface particles under the mechanical actions of agents like wind, rivers, or even glaciers.

In other words, soil erosion is the removal of the most fertile top layer of soil through water, wind, and tillage.

Soil erosion is a consequence of unsustainable land use and other disruptions, such as fire, mining, or intensive agricultural uses. The loss of soil may have grave impacts on the quantity and quality of soil ecosystem services, with severe economic, social, and political implications.

It is a complex process that depends on soil properties, ground grade, vegetation, and the amount of rainfall and its concentration. The misuse of land is one of the most impactful ways of accelerating soil erosion. These changes then have a cascading effect as the loss of fertile topsoil sends millions of tonnes of sediment into lakes and reservoirs, changing ecosystems and impacting agricultural production and water quality.

There are five major types of natural soil erosion:

1) Sheet erosion by water

2) Wind erosion

3) Rill erosion: This happens with heavy rains and usually creates small rills over hillsides.

4) Gully erosion: when water runoff removes soil along drainage lines

5) Ephemeral erosion that occurs in natural depressions

1. Sheet erosion by water

Sheet erosion means that very thin layers or sheets of soil are lost to water. It occurs as a shallow "sheet" of water flowing over the ground surface, which results in the removal of a uniform layer of soil from the soil surface. Sheet erosion occurs when rainfall intensity is reduced along the slope by a consistent flow of rainwater. Another example of sheet erosion is when a layer of freshly ploughed or levelled soil starts to erode evenly from a flow of water.

Water erosion occurs when rain or snowmelt pulls soil from the ground. The more water flows over the land, the more soil particles are pulled out or transported away from land that has no undergrowth. Farm fields that are left barren after crop harvest are particularly vulnerable to water erosion.

The most common example is the erosion of banks by coursing rivers over hundreds of years. This is a natural form of water erosion that would occur with or without human interference.

The effects of soil erosion go far beyond the loss of fertile land. It has led to increased pollution and sedimentation in streams and rivers, clogging these waterways and causing degeneration in fish and other species. Degraded lands are also often less able to hold onto water, which can aggravate flooding. Sustainable land use can help reduce the impacts of agriculture and livestock. It prevents soil degradation and erosion and the loss of valuable land to desertification.

The health of the soil is a primary concern to farmers and the global community, whose livelihoods depend on well-managed agriculture that starts with the earth beneath our feet. While there are many challenges to maintaining healthy soil, there are also solutions and a dedicated group of people who work to update and maintain the soil on which biodiversity springs.

2. Wind Erosion

How Does the Wind Erosion Cause Erosion?

Wind erosion is a natural process that transports soil from one location to another by using the power of the wind. It can cause significant economic and environmental destruction. Wind erosion is a common cause of land degradation in dry and semi-dry grazing lands. It is one of the processes that leads to desertification. Widespread wind erosion occurs when strong winds blow over light-textured soils that have been heavily grazed during periods of drought.

The wind causes erosion by moving the earth around. Therefore, wind erosion can occur anywhere at any time the wind blows. Wind erosion typically occurs in any area where the soil or sand is not compacted or is in a finely granulated state.

Abrupt fluctuations in weather patterns initiate severe wind storms. Wind erosion is the effect of complex interactions among wind intensity, precipitation, surface roughness, soil texture and aggregation, agricultural activities, vegetation cover, and field size. Ploughed soils with low organic matter content and those that are rigorously grazed and crushed are the most susceptible to erosion.

Many people think wind erosion is only a problem in dry regions, but any time there is dry, bare, unprotected soil, wind erosion can happen. Spadework, historically used to prepare fields for planting, creates soil conditions susceptible to wind erosion by breaking down soil aggregation, destroying residue, and drying the soil. Whenever there is no moisture to hold the particles together, wind can separate soil particles and transport them across the fields.

The best way to mitigate wind erosion is to keep the wind off the soil surface by covering the soil surface. Growing vegetation—cash crops and cover crops—shields the soil by keeping the winds higher off the surface. Standing crops continue to function the same way. Flattened crop remains are more effective at reducing soil erosion by water when raindrops are absorbed. The key to reducing erosion is to take up the energy of the wind or water before it can detach soil particles. Windbreaks and other barriers are also effective at keeping the wind away from the soil surface, which reduces soil particle detachment.

Prevention is far more effective than cure when it comes to wind erosion control. The soil surface should be protected with growing vegetation or standing residues. Many producers practise the no-till method, at their planters' risk of wind erosion problems because they detach their residues. Stalk shredding and vertical tillage also increase the chance of wind erosion problems as these operations also detach crop residues. In areas where wind erosion occurs regularly, producers should practise no-tilling between the rows of standing residue and let the residue keep the wind off the soil surface.

This standing residue will also assist in keeping any surface residue from being moved by the wind.

In areas where raindrop impact and water erosion are more of a concern, producers must plant down the old row without moving the residue, so that the residue remains attached and protects the row.

Wind Erosion

65

3. Rill Erosion

Rill erosion happens with heavy rains and usually creates small rills over hillsides.

Rill erosion happens when runoff water forms small waterways as it flows down a slope. These rills can be up to 30 cm deep. It is a type of erosion that results in small, yet well-defined streams.

It happens when water from rainfall does not get absorbed in the soil but runs across it instead. The rills or small channels are affected when water running across the surface of the ground gathers in a natural depression in the soil. Soil erosion begins to happen as the water flows through the depression.

It causes a problem in agriculture as it means loss of topsoil, which comprises most of the nutrients needed to grow crops. Many different organisms live in this soil, which interacts with the minerals in rocks to produce fertile soil. Erosion of any kind, therefore, indicates the washing away of fertile soil from the top layer.

Rill erosion is caused by the concentration of surface water into deeper, faster-flowing channels. As the flow becomes deeper, the velocity increases, and it detaches soil particles from the soil.

It begins to form when the runoff water's shear stress increases. It has the ability to detach soil particles by overcoming the soil's sheer strength in holding onto its compactness. This begins the erosion process as water breaks soil particles free and carries them down the slope.

Courtesy WIKIPEDIA

Source: Rill Erosion photo www.freefoto.com

Once runoff has been initiated, erosion can be prevented by either reducing the water flow velocity or hardening the soil to resist erosion.

Reducing Flow Velocity

Flow velocity can be lessened by either reducing the flow volume or crumpling the soil surface. Increasing surface roughness through the use of grassed waterways and grass filter strips, which work as blockades for soil particles to fall out of suspension. Flow volume can be reduced by not allowing sheet flow to mount up. Techniques such as rip-covered lines and contour drains to prevent runoff build up enough volume and speed to detach and entrain soil particles.

- Rough surface, i.e., grassed waterways, grass filter strips
- Breaking the slope length, i.e., contour drains and ripper covering lines

Hardening the soil surface (to prevent detachment)

Surface soils may be protected from scouring by hardening the surface.

- Compact surface soils.
- Paving and concrete lining.
- rock rip rapping.

4. Gully Erosion

Gully erosion occurs when water runoff removes soil along drainage lines.

How is gully erosion formed?

Gully erosion is an extensive and often-affected form of soil erosion caused by flowing surface water. It consists of open, unsteady channels that have been cut more than 30 cm into the ground. Gully erosion is caused by the interaction of land use, climate, and slope. It happens due to concentrated water flows, either from field runoff and small rills combining together into larger flows or from runoff coming onto the field from a concentrated water source.

It causes severe damage to agricultural lands, which adversely affects agricultural production; it also causes soil loss, increases in surface runoff, lowers soil water-holding capacity, lowers the quality and quantity of water, and lowers the groundwater table.

A gully is formed in three distinct stages: waterfall erosion, channel erosion along the gully bed, and landslide erosion on the gully's banks. Correct gully control measures must be held over according to these development stages.

Causes of gully erosion

Several factors make gully erosion more likely:

• sparse ground cover caused by land clearing, overgrazing, repeated cultivation, fire, rabbits, wild animals, or drought.

• concentrated runoff from steep ground flowing into cleared drainage depressions.

• unstable soils in drainage lines.

• sodic or saline soils: Sodic soils contain a large amount of sodium ions (salt) attached to clay particles.

• intense rainfall

• increased runoff caused by low levels of vegetation cover and/or poor soil infiltration

• unfavourable catchment shape.

Preventing gully erosion

The best way to prevent gully erosion is to maintain good ground cover. Most erosion is caused by occasional heavy rain falling onto areas of poor ground cover.

Actions that prevent gully erosion include:

• maintaining a minimum of 70% ground cover

• keeping a stubble cover of 30% on cultivated areas

• stabilising knick points (points where the channel slope changes sharply) and gully heads

Treating gully erosion

Measures to stabilise gullies must be tailored to the catchment in which the gully occurs. Rainfall, soil type, land use, and catchment dynamics must all be considered.

In general, three strategies are needed to repair gully erosion:

• Modifying the catchment to reduce or redirect runoff.

• stabilising gully heads, floors, and walls with built structures, earthworks, vegetation, or fencing

• reducing stock access to watering points.

Source NSW Department of Planning and Environment

Gully Erosion

Divert surface water can treat soil gully erosion.

Diverting surface water away from the gully is the preliminary step to repairing gully erosion. Reduce or prevent water movement in the gully until the repair is established; otherwise, it will erode any repair work. Diverting water well upslope of the gully using proper surface management that includes spreader banks immediately above the gully head to divert water to a section of stable waterway with a safe receivable area. If this safe area is not available, a stable re-entry location can be created. Spreader banks may also be desired on both sides of long gullies to inhibit surface water from entering the repaired area.

Remove obstacles in the gully.

Plantation or growth of trees and shrubs should be avoided in the repaired gully because these actions create obstacles that can increase erosion by scouring because of heavy flows of water. Dumped machinery, loose rocks, and general rubbish in the gully may also cause more scrubbing

5. Ephemeral gully erosion

Ephemeral erosion usually occurs in natural depressions. Ephemeral gullies are one form of soil erosion where the gullies are much wider than deep. They are formed whenever there is heavy rainfall, mostly on uncultivated arable land. They never go deeper than the tilled layer and can be removed by normal tillage. Hence, as the name "ephemeral gullies" suggests, they are short-lived, temporary, transient, and transitory.

Ephemeral gully erosion

Silent Heroes Who Care For

Our Soil

Our soils are full of life beneath our feet. A place where 1/4th of the Earth's species live, including worms, spiders, nematodes, beetles, springtails and billions of other microorganisms.

Healthy soils are crucial to combating climate change, feeding the planet's population, and preventing flooding and droughts.

These silent heroes of the soil all form a part of our diverse ecosystem and play a fundamental role in keeping soils healthy.

The silent heroes of our soil are:

1. Microorganisms

2. Water bears

3. Bacteria

4. Springtails

5. Protozoa

6. Fungi

7. Worms

It is surprising to note that there are about ten billion microorganisms that can be found in just a quarter of a teaspoon of soil.

1. Microorganisms

Microorganisms are tiny living things. Those are those that are found all around us. They are too small to be seen by the naked eye. They can be found in water, soil, the air and even in human body. The human body is home to millions of these microorganisms, also called microbes. Soil is home to one-fourth of all species on Earth.

Soil-inhabiting nematodes are tiny worm-like creatures. They move slowly between soil particles, putrefying organic matter and recycling nutrients, helping to keep the soil healthy. Nematodes are plentiful creatures on Earth. In fact, just one gram of soil may inhibit more than a million nematodes.

Microorganisms play a positive and very useful role in soil fertility. Usually, people think that microbes are agents of disease, but instead, they perform many other beneficial activities in the biosphere (the portion of the earth consisting of soil, water, and air). The beneficial microorganisms help in the decomposition of toxic waste and other pollutants, and above all, they enhance the soil fertility.

They increase soil fertility by integrating air, minerals, and nitrogenous compounds. They promote plant growth by supplying essential elements and minerals that plants cannot produce on their own.

Microorganisms putrefy organic matter to a simpler form that can be easily accepted by plants.

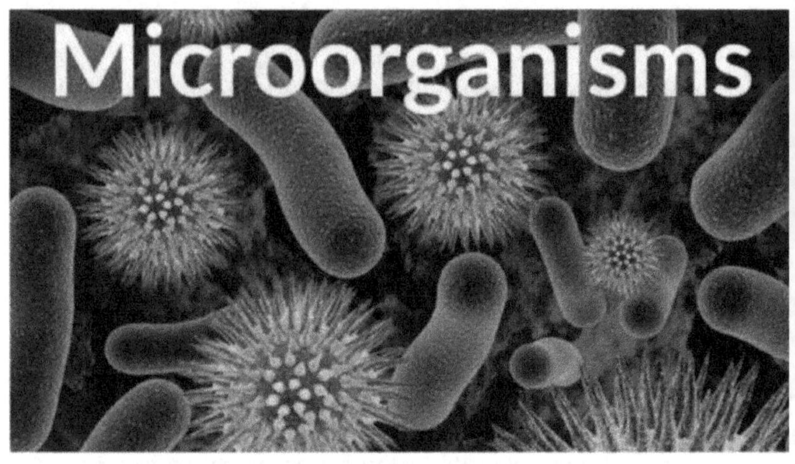

Microorganisms

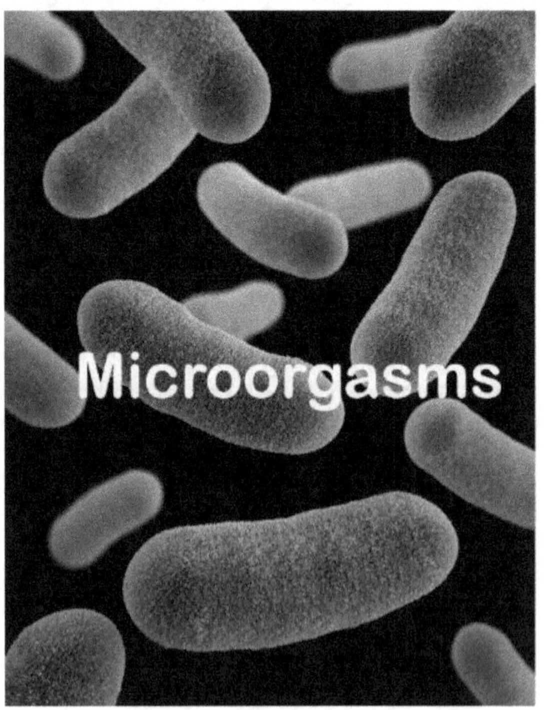

2. Water Bears or Tardigrades

Water bears, or tardigrades, are famous for being one of the most resilient animals on Earth.

They can go up to 30 years without food or water, and can survive at temperatures from freezing to above boiling. They can even survive in the vacuum of space! At less than 1 mm in size, water bears swim inside moss and lichen, consuming plant debris and other organisms as they go, recycling nutrients back into the soil. There are approximately 1200 tardigrade species known to exist on the planet.

Tardigrades can be found in back garden in moss, algae, and soil. They form part of the complex microscopic ecosystem that helps to break down waste, returning nutrients to the soil.

Water Bears or Tardigrades

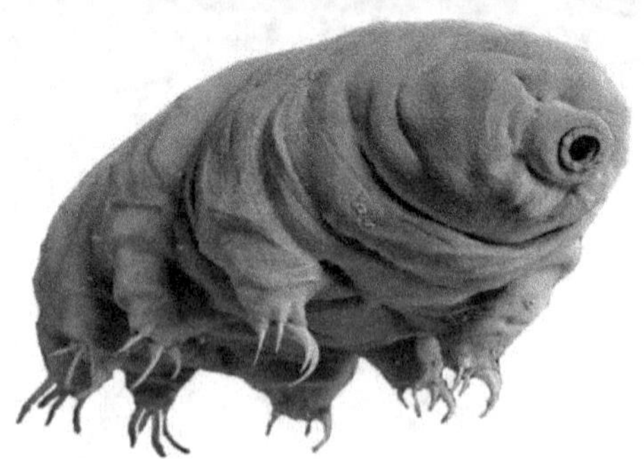

3. Bacteria

Bacteria are essential to living, healthy soil and it is needed to balance the ecosystem.

Most bacteria decompose, helping to convert the energy stored in organic matter into nutrients that feed and enrich other organisms deep in the soil. Some other bacteria are nitrogen-fixing bacteria, converting nitrogen into a useful form for plants, helping them to grow and thrive and facilitating their role in the nitrogen cycle.

Bacteria and microbes live, reproduce, and die at enormous rates. While doing so they release a constant stream of nutrients in plant available form. They gather nitrogen and other nutrients from the soil's organic matter and mineral particles. They reproduce more microbes, and they collect and convert nutrients.

Bacteria putrefies dead organic matter and releases simple compounds into the soil, which can be absorbed by plants. Nitrogen-fixing bacteria fix atmospheric nitrogen and increase the nitrogen content of the soil, which can be readily absorbed by plants, thereby improving the soil health.

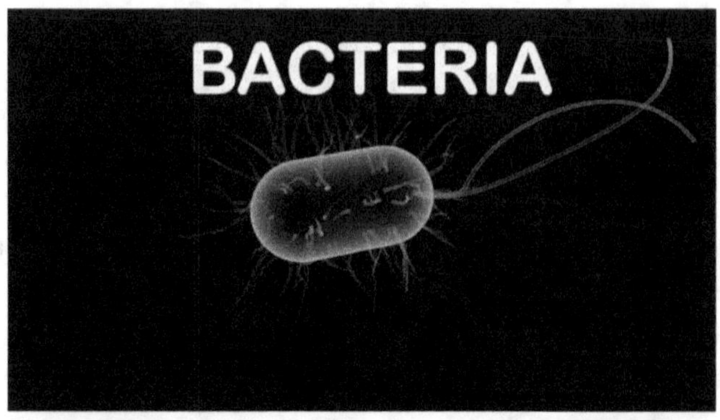

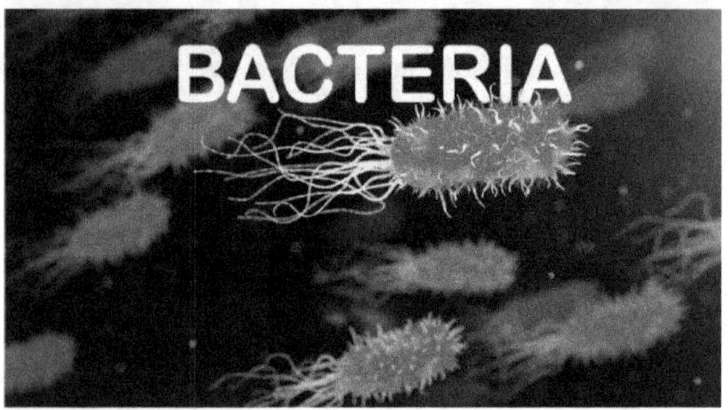

4. Springtails

Springtails are closely related to insects—they have six legs and a head, thorax, and abdomen—but are not insects because of their absence of wings and because they have soft bodies and hidden mouthparts. Springtails are known scientifically as Collembola.

Springtails eat fungi, bacteria, algae, and decaying organic matter and then recycle the nutrients back into the soil. They help most plants by spreading beneficial fungi onto plant roots, helping them thrive.

Springtails live in soil, especially soil adjusted with compost, in leaf litter and organic mulches, and under bark or decaying wood. They feed themselves on decaying plant material, fungi, moulds, or algae. They are also found on the surface of still water or on sidewalks that border flower beds or swimming pools.

They are unique in carrying a jumping organ beneath the abdomen and held in place with hooks. When released, the jumping organ springs free and hits the ground. It forces the animal to leap into the air, hence their common name. Springtails can be found in leaf litter, soil, under bark, sand, under stones, in tree canopies, and even caves, ant, and termite nests in abandoned places. In termite nests, they may control the fungal growth. Most importantly, springtails have been shown to be suitable bio-indicators of environmental change.

SPRINGTAIL

SPRINGTAIL

5. Protozoa

Protozoa are water-borne one-celled animals that live in the water-filled pores and the film of water that surrounds soil particles. They live in the top six inches of the soil. They feed on bacteria, releasing excess nitrogen in a form that is available to the plant roots that surround them.

Protozoa play significant roles in environmental food web dynamics. They scuff on bacteria, thus regulating bacterial populations. They take part in wastewater treatment processes. They assist fertility in soil by releasing nutrients when they digest bacteria.

PROTOZOA

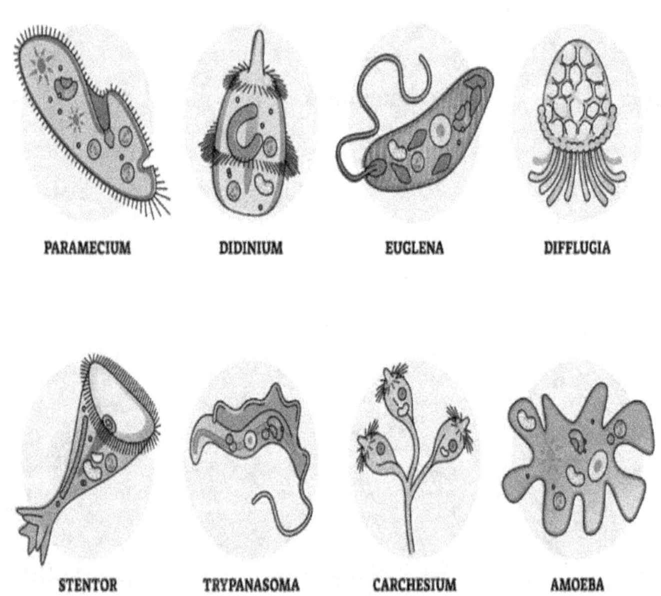

6. Fungi

There's more carbon in our soils than there is in all the world's plants, forests, and atmosphere combined!

Fungi is the plural form of fungus. Most of us think of mushrooms. But these are just the fruiting bodies, and it's a bit like apples on a tree. Most fungi live as an underground network of branching, fusing cells called mycelium. They build up a diverse kingdom of organisms that support the life of our ecosystem. Hidden underground, fungi can spread for kilometres. It creates a huge network that's crucial for soil, and supports plants and trees to communicate; it's sometimes known as the "wood wide web". As carbon capturers, nutrient transporters, and pollution filterers, the role fungi perform in our ecosystem is invaluable. Fungi are 'decomposers'. Fungi obtain nutrition from decaying organic matter such as dead plants, trees, and animals. This process discharges nutrients into the soil, which then become available for plants and trees to absorb. In doing so, they facilitate the "circle of life," cycling nutrients throughout our ecosystem.

Soil erosion is a big concern for farmers. Half the topsoil on our planet has been lost in the last 150 years due to soil erosion and intensive farming. The dense mesh of mycelium in healthy soils holds them together; its networks wind through plant roots and shoots. Without it, soil would be washed away.

Healthy soil can filter out pollutants. Fungi have been found to be amazing cleaners of our soils, filtering out everything from heavy metals to pesticides and even radioactive waste. Protecting and harnessing is the power of fungi.

Overuse of fungicides and artificial fertilisers damages fungi's sensitive mycelium. Deforestation on farmland can also kill the fungi associated with trees and hedges.

By farming in a way that works with nature, known as agro-ecology, we can harness the power of these amazing networks. Instead of using fungicides, organic farming works with "beneficial fungi," which restricts the extinction of favourable fungi. By feeding the soil and the living mycelium within it, and by applying compost, manures, and using cover crops, we can build its fertility in harmony with fungi. In return, farmers are compensated with the amazing ecosystem services that fungi provide—healthier, more buoyant soils and more nutritious crops.

Fungi

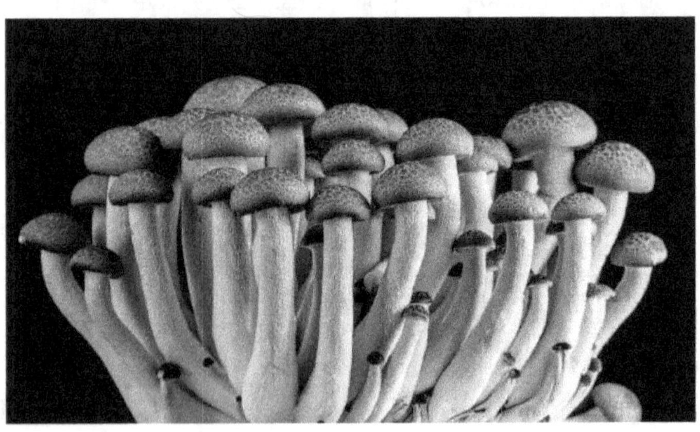

7. Worms

While some people may think them to be the most unattractive of creatures, worms play an important role in the fertility of soil.

These fantastic digging creatures are the living and breathing creatures underneath. They are figuratively called "engineers of the underworld." They are eating and recycling organic matter to keep our soil healthy In fact, the intricate network of tunnels earthworms create below the ground is extremely important to maintaining soil health.

Worms are hungry little creatures, and their diet consists of

- Dead plants
- Fallen leaves
- Fungi, bacteria, and
- Even dead animals.

When they eat, worms disintegrate and recycle this organic matter within the soil, which helps naturally fertilise the earth and ensure it's packed with vital nutrients.

The little mounds sometimes seen on top of the soil are called worm castings (essentially, worm poo!) and are the outcome of this recycling process.

Their casts have a capacity to contain 5 times more nitrogen, 7 times more phosphorus, and 1000 times more beneficial bacteria than the original soil that helps plants thrive.

Worms

Soil Prevent Climate Change

Changes in the quantity of carbon stored in the soil can affect the global carbon cycle and alter carbon dioxide levels in the atmosphere. The decrease in soil carbon may raise greenhouse gas levels in the atmosphere, which contributing to climate change.

Soil is vital and it is often ignored. It is an element of the climate system. It is the second largest carbon store, or 'sink', after the oceans. Depending on the region, climate change might result in more carbon being stored in plants and soil due to vegetation growth or reduce carbon being released into the atmosphere.

Being the second largest natural carbon sink after the ocean, it exceeds forests and other vegetation in its capacity to capture carbon dioxide from the air. The importance of healthy soils is not just for our food production but also to prevent the worst effects of climate change.

Climate change is often seen as something that occurs in the atmosphere. When plants photosynthesise, they pull carbon out of the atmosphere. Atmospheric carbon also affects the soil because carbon that is not used for above-ground plant growth is spread through the roots of a plant. It then deposits carbon in the soil. If it is not spread, this carbon can become stable and remain locked away in the soil.

Healthy soils can thus mitigate climate change.

Soil organic carbon (SOC) is the crucial element that determines soil quality, fertility, agricultural profitability, and atmospheric carbon dioxide (CO_2) fixation. The SOC affects the physio-chemical and biological properties of the soil. It simultaneously improves soil structure, water and nutrient retention capacity.

Higher soil organic carbon (SOC) promotes soil structure, meaning there is greater physical stability. This builds up soil aeration (oxygen in the soil) and facilitates water drainage and retention. It reduces the possibility of soil erosion and nutrient escape.

Loss of soil organic carbon (SOC) content can limit the soil's ability to provide nutrients for sustainable plant production. This may lead to lower harvests and affect food security. Less organic carbon also means less food for the living organisms present in the soil, resulting in a reduction of soil biodiversity.

Nitrogen is very significant and is required for plant growth. It is found in healthy soil, and gives plants the energy to grow and produce fruit or vegetables. Nitrogen is actually considered the most vital component for supporting plant growth. Nitrogen is added to the soil naturally from nitrogen fixation by soil bacteria and legumes and through atmospheric deposition in rainfall. Additional nitrogen is typically supplied to the crop by fertilizers, manure, or other organic materials.

Studies have shown that the addition of nitrogen enhances the stability of soil organic matter (SOM) in a clement forest. The addition of nitrogen enhances SOC stability.

Plants that are deficient in nitrogen have restricted growth, depending on the severity of the deficiency. Leaf growth is inhibited; fresh leaves are inhibited in particular. Longitudinal shoot growth is discouraged, as in nitrogen fixation, which is very significant and is required for plant growth. It is found in healthy soils. It gives plants the energy to grow and produce fruit or vegetables.

Nitrogen is actually considered the most vital component for supporting plant growth. Additional nitrogen is typically supplied to the crop by fertilizers, manure, or other organic materials.

But too much nitrogen, plants produce excess biomass, or organic matter, such as stalks and leaves. It does not produce enough root structure. In extreme cases, plants with very high levels of nitrogen absorbed from soils can kill farm animals that eat them.

Mishandling of land that affects climate change. Mega-droughts or massive floods "significantly limit the ability to re-establish" the soil's ecosystem. When the soil can't be replaced, it ultimately degrades. It contributes to the release of carbon dioxide into the atmosphere.

The increase in atmospheric concentration of carbon-di-oxide from fossil fuel combustion and misuse of land contributes to climate change because of the alarming increase of carbon dioxide in the atmosphere.

A proper strategy has to be identified in order to mitigate the threat of global warming. The industrial revolution has triggered global emissions of carbon (C) due to fossil fuel combustion and due to unsustainable land use change and soil cultivation. Carbon emissions due to land misuse comprise deforestation, biomass burning, conversion of natural to agricultural ecosystems, drainage of wetlands and soil cultivation. Depletion of soil organics has contributed carbon to the atmosphere. Some cultivated soils have lost 1/2 to 2/3 of the original soil organic carbon (SOC) pool with an accumulative loss. The depletion of soil carbon is accentuated by soil degradation and aggravated by land misuse and soil mismanagement. Thus, adoption of restorative land use and recommended management practices on agricultural soils can augment the rate of enrichment of atmospheric carbon while having positive impacts on food security, agro-industries, water quality, and the environment. A considerable part of the depleted soil organic carbon (SOC) pool can be reestablished through the conversion of marginal lands into restorative land uses; adoption of conservation tillage with cover crops and crop residue mulch; nutrient cycling, including the use of compost and manure; and other systems of sustainable management of soil and water resources. Soil carbon sequestration is a truly beneficial strategy. It re-establishes degraded soils, augments biomass production, purifies surface and ground waters.

It reduces the rate of enrichment of atmospheric carbon-dioxide by offsetting emissions due to fossil fuels.

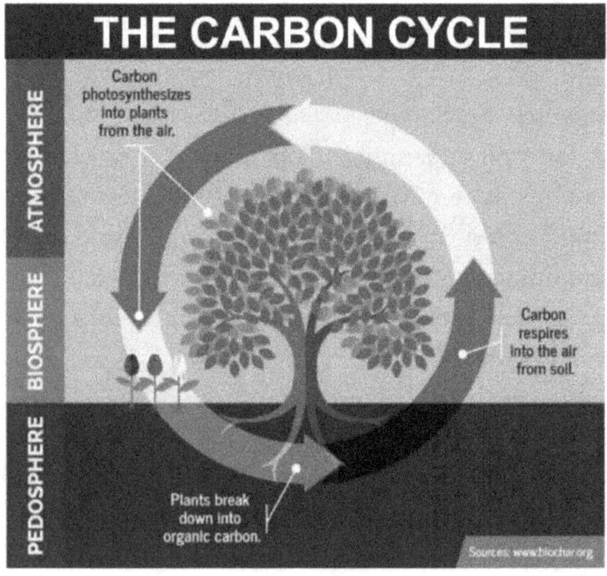

Source: www.biochar.org

Conventional arable cropping with annual crops determined by ploughing and breaking up degrades larger soil accumulations that cause reduction in soil organic carbon (SOC). The urgent need to increase the SOC content of arable soils to improve their functioning and reduction of atmospheric carbon dioxide. Elimination of atmospheric carbon dioxide by reintroducing grasslands into long-term conventional arable fields will uplift the soil condition. However, the effects of short-term grasslands on total SOC accumulation have sometimes been misleading.

Soil aggregation is said to be important for carbon storage. The effects of arable-to-ley conversion on cambisol soil after three years of ley on concentrations are remarkable. The stocks of SOC and nitrogen and their distributions in different sized water-stable aggregates have increased. It has been found that SOC stocks (0–7 cm depth) rose from 20.3 to 22.6 Mg per hectare in the arable-to-ley conversion.

Soil organic carbon (SOC) is the crucial element that determines soil quality, fertility, agricultural profitability, and atmospheric carbon dioxide (CO_2) fixation. The SOC affects the physio-chemical and biological properties of the soil. It simultaneously improves soil structure, water and nutrient retention capacity. Higher soil organic carbon (SOC) promotes soil structure, meaning there is greater physical stability. This builds up soil aeration (oxygen in the soil) and facilitates water drainage and retention. It reduces the possibility of soil erosion and nutrient escape.

How Can Saving Soil Contribute to Reversing Climate Change?

• Restoring and re-establishing forest lands.

• Bringing the soil under shade and increasing its organic content and promoting soil absorption

• Stepping up soil health that keeps carbon underground

• Keeping sufficient natural spaces that act as powerful defence mechanisms against the impact of climate change. For example, green spaces and healthy riverside areas can significantly cool the temperatures of a given place.

• Capturing carbon in the air by converting arable lands to grasslands could increase the carbon content in the soil.

• Reinstating land ecosystems and increase soil fertility that in turn prevents soil erosion hence alleviating possibilities of flood.

• Refreshing dying biodiversity that prevents soil regeneration. 80% of insect biomass have disappeared, and almost 27,000 species of life forms are approaching extinction.

• Instituting national policies and actions towards increasing organic content in soil.

• Reducing water scarcity as depleted soils cannot regulate or absorb water flow.

————————

To make all these possible, just a one-man show would not do justice. It needs this world to be one and monopolise this responsibility for making this planet happily liveable.

www.ingramcontent.com/pod-product-compliance
Lightning Source LLC
LaVergne TN
LVHW011036200726
843509LV00011B/1292